MW00413336

Sweaty Mess Sex Games: 50+ Creative, Kinky, and Hot Ways to Spice Up Your Sex Life.

Just Say No to Vanilla Sex!

By Amber Cole, Sex Coach

Sweaty Mess Sex Games

Table of Contents

Sweaty Mess Sex Games

Introduction

As a sex coach, I often work with couples that have completely lost the spark in their relationships.

It's usually neither person's fault, and the fact that they are coming to see me is a truly positive sign. While there are a host of psychological and self-esteem issues involved in a degrading sex life, I can tell you something that many therapists and counselors seem to disregard.

Fun.

Sex has simply stopped being fun and enjoyable. It feels more like a chore you need to complete at the end of the day, like balancing your checkbook, or taking out the trash (this is an actual analogy I've heard from someone).

Just imagine if you loved playing baseball your entire life. If you stopped enjoying it, why would you keep playing it? There would be no reason. You'd stop and find something else to enjoy or occupy your time.

That's the amazing value of learning and experimenting with sex games.

Much of the time, people struggling with their sex life start to put pressure on themselves, which leads to expectations. This can be detrimental because you're thinking about the expectations more than the sex itself! Sex games take the focus off the sex itself, and allow you to inject fun back into your sex life. When you have something else to think about and try to achieve that also happens to create sexual tension and arousal, before you know it, you'll be having sex as a byproduct of the game.

A particular set of clients were named John and Felicia. They described a sex life where they had sex only once a month and were both dissatisfied with it, but didn't know how to improve it and re-ignite the spark they once had.

It turned out that they were so busy they stopped prioritizing each other. I recommended a simple sex game involving hiding index cards and commands (that you'll learn later). It was silly and they were skeptical at first, but over the next week, they found that it worked wonders in creating desire and arousal. It was fun again.

Maybe you're on the opposite side of the spectrum and you have zero issues with your sex life and just like to be creative and crazy.

Whatever the case may be, welcome to my world. I hope you enjoy it.

Come with me, won't you?

Sweaty Mess Sex Games

Chapter 1. Why Sex Games?

An entire book devoted to sex games? You might be asking why this is necessary.

If you've been in a relationship that's like 99% of relationships, then your sex life is probably a bit less exciting and thrilling than it once was. In a word, it becomes routine, especially if you are living together with your lover.

In the beginning, you were in the honeymoon phase. That was when you couldn't get enough of them and their mere smell was intoxicating for you. We ignore our other friends and obligations – even work – to spend time with this person, and sexual expression and release is a big part of that.

This is a result of novelty and things being new between the two of you. It's a wonderful feeling that we love to bask in forever, but that is impossible for the majority of us.

If you're still in the honeymoon phase, then you may not need this book yet, because the slightest whiff of their aroma will be enough to make you quiver.

As you become more accustomed to someone, the honeymoon phase inevitably dies down because you start to see your lover as a person, and not just a concept of a being that you can have sex with. You see them as a three-dimensional person with flaws and faults, and traits that may get on your nerves.

You have to succumb to other obligations and re-integrate yourself back into your life while balancing another priority: your partner. As if you didn't have enough responsibilities! There are so many people you need to catch up with! Your time spent with your lover might only be one or two date nights a week because that's all you have the energy for otherwise.

The point of this is show that despite our best efforts, our sex lives can grow stale quite easily. In some best case scenarios, sex can be like a chore we endure at the end of the day when we really just want to catch an extra fifteen minutes of sleep. In the worse case scenarios, we live in dead bedroom situations – sexless relationships – with partners who function like roommates. None of this is good.

The bottom line is this: the partners have forgotten just how great and fun sex can be. That's why this is an entire book devoted to sex games to take your sex life to the next level, or reinvigorate it completely. It can take you from strangers who pass each other in the night, to that couple who can't keep their hands off each other.

The first reason is re-discovering your partner.

Rediscovery

This is the first reason sex games are so beneficial for your sex life. Often when we drift from our partners sexually, or have decreased interest in them sexually, it's because we feel distance from them in general. In other words, it's not necessarily a sex problem, it's a relationship problem.

You may be well aware that sex is just one of the symptoms of an underlying cause. Regardless, sex games will help you tackle both the symptom and the underlying cause.

Sex games force you to laugh, work, and think together towards a common goal. It's this simple act of spending time engaging with someone in this way, and having fun that many people have forgotten. Imagine you are reading about one of the sex games from later in this book, and you are gasping from laughter while trying to figure out how to best adapt it to your situation. When's the last time you did that with your partner? That's the rediscovery of them as the fun-loving person you fell in love with, not the person who works too much and sometimes makes a mess in the bathroom sink.

Having fun together leads to rediscovery, and sex games are nothing if not fun.

Novelty

Of course, the novelty and allure of something new is also a major part of sex games. This is the feeling of first-time discovery rather than rediscovery.

Your sex life might be boring simply because it's boring. It might be too routine. You might want to try out kinks and fetishes that you saw in pornography. You might not even know what you like, so you want to try out as much as possible.

The pleasure of novelty in sex is well-documented both scientifically and anecdotally. For example, are you more likely to be turned on when your partner has new sexy underwear, or when they whip out sexy underwear that you've seen dozens of times? That same lust for novelty is transferred over to the sex itself.

Sex games allow and push you to experience things you never would have thought of. If imagination isn't your strong suit, just leave that to me. I'll take care of that part and give you more than you can handle! You never know when you might see something that catches your eye and uncovers a trigger for your best orgasms. If you have the same type of sex with the same routines and same lack of creativity over and over, it's easy to understand why your sex life is suffering. Try out some games and make it spicy and exciting again.

Tension

What is tension in this context? Tension is the feeling of anticipation for something that motivates you toward it. Sexual tension is created when you have the desire, but can't necessarily take care of it in that moment.

Sexual tension is an important part of a fulfilling sex life. Without it, you likely have no desire.

Sex games create sexual tension because that's how I've designed them! They are designed to open your mind and do something where sex might not even be the end goal. But, without your realization, you are more turned on and aroused by the game, until the sexual tension boils over and you just want to rip your partner's clothes off. Take the most obvious example of a sensual massage. Your partner orders you to strip naked for a full body massage and soaks your body in oil. They also strip naked. The point there isn't necessarily to have sex, but once the hands start gliding everywhere, it's probably where it will lead.

Effort

Perhaps above all else, sex games represent intentional time and effort spent in the pursuit of a better sex life. This is the most important part of a fulfilling sex life – the notion that you must work at it, and it's not a given for compatible people. Many people assume that if their sex life with their partner is not naturally orgasmic, then it's a sign of the wrong partner.

Wrong! A healthy sex life, and consistently fulfilling and remarkable sex, is not something that just happens by accident. It would be like assuming an extremely muscular person just happened to end up that way. No, it was the result of a lot of work, planning, and most importantly, time spent honing their craft. That's the approach towards sex that we need to have, because expecting it to be great without working at it doesn't make much sense.

Great sex is something to achieve: a goal, not something that is a naturally given.

In "How Implicit Theories of Sexuality Shapes Sexual and Relationship Well-Being," Maxwell et al. demonstrated that there were essentially two types of people. There were people who had sexual *growth* beliefs, and there were people with sexual *destiny* beliefs.

What is the difference between the two? Those with a growth belief imagined sexual satisfaction to be honed like a skill, which required hard work and a certain amount of time, and those with a destiny belief imagined sexual satisfaction to be capped and pre-destined with a certain partner, and that there was nothing they could do to improve it save getting a different partner.

Guess which group showed consistently higher satisfaction in their sex lives? The sexual growth belief group – those who saw sex as a task to master, and subsequently spent time to improve and master it. It shows that people who believe in the power of change will be motivated and have something to work toward, which benefits their sex lives. They are rewarded by discovery, exploration, discussion, and communication, whereas those with the sexual destiny belief won't engage in any of that.

The other group, on the other hand, will do nothing to improve themselves. They believe their sex life is as-is, and see a sexual problem, inadequacy, misunderstanding, or deficiency as a sign that they are with the wrong partner. Instead of trying to fix the problem, they see it as a black and white spectrum. If the sex is great, the relationship is right; if the sex is mediocre or bad, the relationship is wrong.

Guess which group probably tried sex games and exploration far more?

Sweaty Mess Sex Games

Chapter 2. Common Mistakes and Barriers

Even if you're squarely in agreement that sex games and exploration have a place in your sex life, it doesn't mean you're ready to actually do them. There are many obstacles we may face in fulfilling our sexual desires. Many are related to our partners, but many are also simply related to us.

Do you want to jump into a sex game tonight? Not so fast! These are some of the issues you will have to overcome, or at least address.

Insecurity

Some people are pushed away from sex because they don't feel good about themselves. This can take many forms, and it's certainly not gender specific.

You might not want to have sex if you feel like you've gained weight and your body image is poor. You might not feel sexy or attractive even taking your shirt off when this happens. Naturally, you aren't going to want to expose yourself to someone else if this is the case. It can also stem from anything physical that you are self-conscious or displeased about, such as a haircut or even a new pimple.

You can also face a loss of confidence through mental and emotional factors, such as losing your job or performing poorly during a meeting. All of these things contribute to feeling bad about yourself, and they can persist for days, even months.

Another contributor to insecurity can be related to your partner, specifically if they turn you down for sex in a negative or harmful manner. This can color your perception about sex and make you feel undesirable. To stop that negative feedback, you might simply stray away from sex and feel bad about it. Even rejecting someone sexually multiple consecutive times can be harmful to someone's sense of self-esteem.

Insecurity can take many forms, and it takes a certain degree of security and confidence to be completely naked and in the mood.

Lack of Prioritization

If you think you can just set aside twenty minutes at the end of your day for a quick tryst, you are incredibly wrong, and that is the mindset that makes your sex life unfulfilling.

You simply don't prioritize it. You don't make time for it, and yet you expect it to be a great experience every time. That's like expecting to be a professional athlete while making fitness your last priority of the day, one that is often skipped and ignored. It doesn't make sense.

If you feel like you need to block out time on your schedule for sex, that's fine. It may not be the most romantic, but that's something you can deal with later. You need to prioritize sex higher than reading the next chapter of your leisure book, or watching the next episode of your television show. Before you know it, you might not want to interrupt your bedtime reading, and it's been two months since you last had sex. At that point, inertia has taken hold, and things are just downhill from there.

It's not necessarily being selfish, it's just a matter of expectations. You can't expect a great experience if you don't give it the proper attention it needs, and this includes things like paying attention to your partner and thinking about them in a sexual manner. If you don't put in the effort, they likely will not either, and where will that leave you?

Lack of Communication

Many people are uncomfortable talking sex, even with the people they are having sex with. In my view, if you have already spread-eagled naked for someone, it doesn't get more vulnerable and revealing than that. Voicing your desires should be an easier step, but for most of us, it's not.

What keeps you from exploring sexually is the fact that you can't communicate about sex in a sincere manner. You can't talk about what you like, what you want, and what you don't like without feeling self-conscious and like you will be severely judged. You need to be able to communicate without feeling judged, but also make sure you aren't conveying judgment that would prevent someone else from communicating their desires.

If you are too embarrassed to say what you want, sex games are going to be very difficult for you to complete. If you are too shy to discuss sex, or you have a repressed attitude and beliefs about it, try doing it for your partner's happiness. The simple ability to talk about sex is something most people lack, and it leads to people tolerating acts they hate, while skipping acts they love.

That is wholly unnecessary, and all it takes is a few seconds of gritting your teeth and having the words tumble out of your mouth. If you are the first to move, you will inspire your partner to also open up.

In a similar vein, communication as a whole is important. Specifically, conflict resolution and how you deal with disagreements in sex or otherwise. If conflict is not handled with respect, it will bleed into the sexual attraction.

23

No Tension

As I mentioned previously, sexual tension is the anticipation of sex that motivates you toward it. There are many ways to create sexual tension besides sex games. Being more romantic is one of the easiest ways that you may have lost sight of. You can also praise, touch, hug, kiss, and flirt more. These are all things that are easy to fall by the wayside and be forgotten, but remember how you acted when you first got with your partner? You initiated sexual tension constantly with the idea of sex, and it led to sex. Without it, there is no mystery or allure surrounding sex.

Spontaneity Versus Reactivity

One of the final barriers to better sex is not understanding how the libidos of males and females differ. No, this isn't to say that men are entirely more obsessed with sex. For all intents and purposes, we can assume that female and male libidos are equal. The difference, however, is in how they are displayed and what they do with them.

Male sexuality is spontaneous, which means that it may be constantly in the background, ready to erupt at any moment. They are ready to have sex spontaneously, without prior provocation or arousal. Studies have confirmed this, and anecdotally it seems very true.

Female sexuality, on the other hand, is said to be reactive. It is no more or less, but it requires a prior arousal or stimulation to get them in the mood. They may not feel aroused or sexually alert walking down the street, but once they are kissed or touched, they are in the same boat as men. Socially, of course, this is also ingrained in us. Men are seen as the aggressive conquerors that seduce women, while women are seen as temptresses that make men unable to control themselves.

What does this mean for you?

It's a matter of having proper expectations. If you are a man and expect the woman to initiate sex constantly, you might not win that battle. They will need you to initially help them along. If you are a woman and your man isn't initiating sex with you much, you might need to get yourself started! Having greater knowledge about how each gender perceives sex is beneficial to better sex.

Boring

The other issues might not be an issue for you – you just might not have any imagination of what to do! Your sex is fine but boring, because you are boring and uncreative.

You either can't imagine how the parts fit together in the pornography you've seen, or you are overwhelmed and don't know where to get started with fetishes, kinks, and sex games. Nothing seems realistic, or they seem too complex to accomplish in the heat of the moment.

If this is the case, then this is definitely the right book for you.

Chapter 3. Getting Textual

With the rise of technology, you'd be hard-pressed to find even a teenager that hasn't used their phone or computer for sexual purposes. I'm talking about dirty emails, phone sex, texting, sexting, sending nude photos, and "cybersex."

These are great tools for your sexually adventurous sex games. If you want to break it down, they are ways for you to build anticipation and communicate without being present. This can be powerful, because previously, we could only foreplay in person, while touching. Technology presents another layer of fun that we should all be taking advantage of. This is doubly true if you're in a long-distance relationship, and communicating through technology is the only real option.

Here are a few was to get technical so you can get more sexual.

Send and Forget

We all know what sexting is, right? If you don't, sexting is just sending sexual messages or pictures through text. Some people use text, while others use messaging apps that protect your privacy better, such as Whatsapp, Kik, or Snapchat.

Here's the twist. You are going to be texting someone like you normally do, and then every one to two texts, you will send them something dirty. Then, you will act like nothing happened, and don't acknowledge the texts you send. Just act shocked at your partner's reaction, and play innocent and dumb.

For example:

M: What do you want to do for dinner?
W: Maybe that Chinese place down the block?

W: I want to feel your cock hit the back of my throat.
M: Wait... what? Now?
W: What do you mean? You don't like Chinese?
M: I mean about sucking my cock.
W: No clue what you mean. I'll call ahead.
W: [nude photo]

And so on.

If they start to text dirty, ignore them and act shocked that they are being so explicit, while you get even dirtier in your subsequent text.

The key is to spark an interest by innocently bringing the topic of sex up, then getting them invested by making them figure out what you're doing. This works best if you do it throughout the day because you will be able to build tension for that long. The first step to sex is to get sex on the mind. You get sex on the mind, but then you also act oblivious. It's the ultimate push and pull routine that can drive someone wild.

Skype Remote Control

This is for the more seasoned long-distance sexpert. There are two levels here.

The first level is to mutually masturbate over Skype, or another type of video chat, so your partner can see all the action. You might have done this before. The easiest way to do this is to start dirty talk by telling them what you want to do to them, and what you want them to do to you in that moment. You continue to narrate what you visualize happening as they begin to touch themselves more. This isn't the game.

The second step is the game.I Instead of normal dirty talk where you narrate what you like and what you want to do to them, you control the speed of their actions. For example, the female can control how quickly the male strokes his cock, and the male can control how quickly the female rubs her clitoris. They are each other's remote controls. Take turns and direct each other on how fast to go, keeping in mind how they normally orgasm.

You can go fast then stop completely for a few seconds.

You can alternate fast and slow for five seconds each.
You can go fast until the brink of orgasm, then back away.
You can tease them slowly for a while, with random bouts of fast motion.

The possibilities are endless. You don't even have to state what you are planning to do. Just tell your partner how quickly you want them to go, and you will be turned on if they listen to you. Then, encourage them to do the same for you.

The Errand Tease

This is a great sex game that you may not be able to do that often, but will provide a huge impact for the times that you can! The reason you may not be able to do this so frequently is because it depends on taking your partner by surprise. Here's how it works.

You send your partner out for a short errand that will take under one hour. You can also initiate this game roughly one hour before you are to meet with them in public or private.

After you send them out, or otherwise know there is a set amount of time before you will see them, start bombarding them with sexy texts and pictures. Tell them what you'd like them to do to you, how hard, and in what position. The emphasis here is on you telling them and showing them through pictures. Tell them what you are going to be wearing and what you will do the moment they walk through the door. You are taking the lead in painting the picture and setting the stage. Ideally, they will look at their phone absent-mindedly while they buy milk, and be assaulted by the way you are teasing them.

They will reply aroused and intrigued. Build off of that and continue to paint the scene when they are involved. You are building an immense amount of tension by using the errand as a boundary, and it will drive them crazy for the remainder of the time before they arrive.

This same game can work whenever you know you will see them in a set amount of time. The tension might be even higher if you do this before you meet in public, because then you won't be able to act on it – or will you?

Build a Scene

This is something you might have done as a child. You are going to build an erotic sex scene via text, one sentence at a time. That is, you are going to alternate sentences in building the scene, and you will see where it ends up.

The scene doesn't necessarily have to involve the two of you, it can be about two other characters. That doesn't detract from how arousing this will be. Tell your partner you are going to play this game. There are many ways you can start to play – you just need to set the initial stage.

- "I walk into the backyard and you are lying in a lawn chair reaching down your pants and playing with yourself."
- "We are suddenly on a candle-lit beach with no one else around us."
- "We are in the co-ed sauna at the gym together in only towels, and no one else is around."

From there, you will both add to the scene, but focus on the actions of the characters involved. Don't be afraid to be the one to move the scene into the next phases of sex, for example, from foreplay to oral, from oral to penetration, from penetration to orgasm. You might have to be the one to do it and keep things moving.

Depending on how proficient you get at writing erotica, so to speak, you can transition this to two sentences or even a small paragraph each when it's your turn. You might discover a hidden talent!

Multiple Choice

This is a great game that will require amounts of creativity and quick thought on your part.

The premise is that you text your partner a series of options for what you could do in that exact moment, and then your partner chooses the one they like best. For example, if you are both in your respective homes, you could text:

"I'm here with my hand on my cock stroking myself thinking of you. I need distraction.

34

Should I look at pictures of you, take a shower, put my cock away, or send you a picture of what I'm doing?"

Make sure you make it easy for them to answer and continue the conversation. If you are in public and they are home, or vice versa, you could text something like:

"I'm in public, but I want you in my throat. Should I go to the bathroom to find some release for myself, get another drink, or send you some upskirt photos?"

Notice that among the choices, one or two are very sexual and move the interaction forward in that manner. There is at least one neutral, non-sexual option in case your partner isn't necessarily in the mood at the moment. The Multiple Choice sex game gives people the chance to engage and take it as far as they want. Keep giving your partner choices until it becomes very obvious what they want, and the hot sex will naturally follow this game.

There is a variation on this game where you text your partner what you will do the next time you see each other. For example, if you are going to meet for dinner later that night, you could text something like:

"What do you want to do after dinner? We can dress up and go to a nice jazz bar, go to your place and take a bath together where I'll swallow your cum, or we can go dancing and I won't wear underwear. What do you want to do?"

You can also ask your partner to give you a set of choices so you can pick. Just make sure to follow through on your decisions the next time you see them!

Treasure Hunt

This is where you leave something sexy or sexual behind for your partner to find. Suppose you spent the night at your partner's home, and you left him a pair of your used underwear (which drives him crazy). It can also be a new sex toy, a piece of lingerie, handcuffs, a leather collar, lubrication, or anything that you know they enjoy or will arouse them.

Give them a hunt to find them! After you leave, text them you've left them something special for them to find. They will naturally ask where it is, but you need to restrict the types of questions they can ask, otherwise it will be too easy for them to find.

Only allow them to ask yes or no questions to prolong this tease, and if they can't find the item you've left within twenty questions, make it known that they will be required to perform a series of services on you the next time you meet.

Secret Agent

This one can also be done through email. The premise is to send your partner a series of texts with a set of instructions that they cannot acknowledge or reply to. It's as if you are sending classified information, hence the name of the game. This works best if you are set to meet that night in private. If you can book a hotel room for this game, that's even better.

The first step is to send your partner a series of rules as follows in one big text message:

1. You are not allowed to respond or acknowledge anything I send you today

through text. You may only respond "yes" or "no" when I ask for a response.
2. I will send you pictures or a story for you to masturbate to every few hours. (Every time you do this, ask them if they are masturbating.)
3. You may NOT orgasm. (This is to make them feel teased.)
4. You will take pictures every time you masturbate. Send them to me.
5. We will meet at 7 p.m. at [insert hotel name and room number if possible, otherwise just one of your residences]
6. I will call you 10 minutes before we meet. You will tell me how it felt to touch yourself all day and how much you want me to touch, lick, and fuck you. You will be touching yourself during the call.
7. Reply "Yes" when you read this and do not acknowledge it.

Then, proceed to text normally but be more affectionate than usual. This is to make them feel valued and loved, and that the sex isn't a purely lusty, physical act.

Send your partner three stories about what you want to do to them and how hot they make you, accompanied by pictures of you touching and pleasuring yourself. Remind them of the rules every time. By the time you see each other face to face, you aren't even going to say anything. You'll just tear each other's clothes off.

Why does this work? Because you are controlling everything and restricting what they are able to do. It's the ultimate tease. Even if they want more, they aren't allowed to get it. All they can do is become more aroused throughout the day, thinking about what's happening and the stories you are sending. There are also elements of domination and power, which are sexy no matter how you identify in the relationship. Just being at someone else's whim and being told what to do are sexy. Novelty, of course, is strong here as well.

It's a situation they have likely never encountered before. They may never have been under a set of rules for texting, and had a secret, sexual conversation and a normal one simultaneously. That's part of the magic here – it's like they are hiding it, which makes it feel slightly forbidden and taboo. That's just hot and will lead to a great time.

Sweaty Mess Sex Games

Chapter 4. Teasing Games

Hopefully at this point in the book, you realize the arousing value of teasing, tension, and anticipation. It's one of the main factors of how you will get rock-hard or soaking wet. It puts sex into the forefront of your brain and doesn't allow you to lose focus.

It would be helpful to define in a more cement fashion what we're aiming for when we tease someone. We want to arouse someone, then withhold sex, basically. You convey the possibility, then withdraw the invitation. You pull them closer and then subtly push them away. You are hot for them, then suddenly neutral towards them.

You may recognize these as tactics that work while pursuing someone in the dating scene. They function in exactly the same way. When you plant the idea of sex, it has been confirmed that teasing is essentially for the purpose of making someone want you sexually.

The psychology of teasing isn't cruel or malicious, as long as you don't have the intent to be cruel and truly withhold yourself. There must always be a payoff when you tease, otherwise you are just tormenting someone. You can make it appear as if there won't be a payoff, but that could very well all be an illusion. With the goals of creating anticipation and interest in mind, let's delve into some sex games that will tease your partner to no end.

Commercial Breaks

This will work best when you are watching a television show that has commercials, but it's fine for movies as well. Here's how it works.

Every time the show goes to commercial, you start ravishing your partner who is probably sitting next to you. Kiss them, grope them, take them in your mouth, rip their clothes off, and whisper dirty talk to them. Do this with increasing intensity during each commercial break, then stop suddenly when the show or movie comes back. Don't discuss what you are doing beforehand. Just ravage them intermittently.

They will want to continue, but give them a wry smirk and say you will continue later, don't worry. By the time the show ends, your partner will either be so hard they are light-headed, or so wet they are drowning in their panties. The instant the show ends, immediately pounce on your partner and see the fruits of your labor.

You will have been teasing them anywhere from 30-60 minutes. That is going to have an effect on them, and you might not even make it to the end. They might even beg you, but hold out until the end of the show or movie for greater anticipation if you can. This is the quintessential demonstration of what teasing looks like – you are giving them all the green lights, then giving them a red light. They are revving their engine at the red light for minutes, which makes them extremely ready and primed to go once they are allowed to.

You can do this any time there are breaks in what the two of you are doing together. For example, watching sports, or listening to a radio show or podcast. Use it during a study break, even. The point is to trigger intense arousal for a few minutes, then let the arousal simmer in the background.

Dead Fish

This is also known as the statue or the corpse. This is a great teasing sex game because you literally stop all action and let the other person take charge, or simply let things cool down momentarily.

Here's how it works.

You are getting hot and heavy during foreplay. Your pants are off, and you are doing oral or receiving it. You might even be in the intercourse phase. Then, you simply lie on your back and tell the other person to use you. You will barely move, but tell your partner to use whatever means necessary to make you orgasm. You lie there like the proverbial dead fish who is bad at sex, only you are doing it on purpose to give them a challenge and change roles.

Only sexual acts: no torture or tickling during this time. This is a great game because it forces your partner to take charge, and it allows you to reap the rewards. You can do the same thing in reverse – tell them to lay on their backs like a dead fish while you try to make them orgasm in any way possible.

A slight variation on this is called the Sleeping Fish – where you close your eyes and pretend you are sleeping. Your partner has the same task of giving you an orgasm in whatever way possible, and arranging your body in that way. You can also add the wrinkle of making it seem like they don't want to wake you up, so they have to be quiet and sneaky with their movements.

Mutual Masturbation

This is just what it sounds like. You are both masturbating right in front of each other, but not allowed to touch each other. Where this is different is that it's also a contest – you see how many times you can get to the edge of orgasm and back off.

Both of you are edging and taking yourself to the brink, and the person who orgasms first loses – but also wins. It's a continual tease, but you're doing it to yourself, and watching your partner as well.

Note Master

This game is great for teasing, because you get to tease them in whatever situation they're in. Leave notes everywhere. And I mean everywhere. Write on mirrors after you shower. Do everything possible to leave as many sexually charged messages as possible for your partner to see when you're not there.

Pay special attention to leave notes they will see in public, such as their wallet, purse, briefcase, or car.

It's sufficient to just write on index cards, or anything that can hold one or two sentences of text. What will you write? Focus on what you'd like to do to them, what you enjoy from them, your favorite acts, your favorite shared sexual memories, your fantasies, how you want to have sex the next time you meet,

46

what they should do to make you orgasm harder, what they think about when they masturbate, and what the last thing was to make you wet or hard.

Make it so that your note of sexual arousal breaks up the monotony of their day, and makes them crack a smile when they are paying for their burrito. Seed their day with sexual tension and put them in the mood from the start of their day.

You don't need to mention that you're leaving notes for them. They will figure that all out by themselves very quickly. Just make sure to leave one or two in easy-to-find locations so they will recognize that the game is afoot.

This game can actually take days or weeks to finish because of the possibility of where you can leave notes. It's a good thing!

Third Base

We all know that exhibitionism can be extremely sexy and arousing. What happens when you pair that with another challenge – getting to third base, otherwise known as oral sex?

This game is all about the thrill of the challenge, but it's relatively benign. Having full-on sex in public is a bit of a challenge that is too far out of most people's zones of comfort. The most thrilling games push you just a bit out of that comfort zone, and also feel realistic and doable.

This sex game involves sneaking around corners, locking doors, looking over your shoulder, and high amounts of adrenaline. Imagine how quick and alert you'll have to be to look for the dark corners where you can drop to your knees. It's a huge thrill.

Better yet, you can turn this into a challenge for you as a couple. How many can you do in one day, alternating who is the giver and who is the receiver? You can shoot for a goal of five times during a holiday party, or ten times during a trip to the mall. Get creative with where you can have oral sex in public, and it will translate to your private encounters.

Porno Pleasure

What kind of book would this be if I didn't mention anything about pornography?

Pornography can be a great tool for initiating foreplay, learning about your interests, and getting creative with your partner.

Pornography is literally experiencing another couple having sex right there with you. As a general side note, I'm a big fan of integrating pornography into your sex play. There are so many things you can do with it besides, of course, teasing.

First, you can imitate exactly what you see in the porn you are watching.

This includes everything from the positions, noises, moans, groans, and facial expressions. Treat the pornography as an instruction video for exactly what you should do next. You'll see that being an adult film actor isn't as easy a job as you think it is! Your task for this sex game is to mimic the actors as closely as possible, and the person who can't keep up with the video is deemed the loser. What happens to the loser? They have to pleasure the winner in any method of the winner's choice for ten minutes.

Second, you can use porn as part of your foreplay, and that's how you use it to tease.

You can think of this game as a lesser version of the first version. Here, you mimic what's happening in the video, but without penetrative sex. You may use your hands and your mouth, but no penetration will occur here. If you think you won't be able to control yourself, have both partners keep their underwear on. It's the ultimate tease, because you are being stimulated by your partner, by the porn, and most importantly, by the fact that you are going through all these positions without actual sex. It will drive you both crazy.

If you want to mix things up a bit more, you can navigate to your favorite streaming porn site and type in a random letter. After the search results load, click on the sixth result and act out what's happening in that video. Immediately slip into the character.

30 On, 60 Off

There are a few ways to play this game! Perhaps the more fun way is to not tell your partner that you are playing it, so they get a sense of teasing and sexual frustration when dealing with you!

The premise of this game is to go hot and heavy for thirty seconds, and then completely stop and lay off for sixty seconds. Over a few rounds, this is going to build up into something that you simply can't control, and the rest will flow naturally.

You can set a timer or just eyeball it. For thirty seconds, you will be kissing passionately, groping, pinning against the wall, and telling them how hot they make you. Then, for the next sixty seconds, you are going to get deeply focused on something else, ignore them as best as you can, and pretend like it never happened. That's one round.

After a few rounds, don't simply stop after thirty seconds, and the other person will have built up a tremendous reservoir of lust for you.

As I mentioned, there are a couple of other ways to play this that might seem somewhat more organic and natural – one of them being the commercial break method described earlier.

Danger Zones

I saved the best for last because I feel that this is the ultimate teasing sex game.

There are two versions. The first version is to view your hands and mouth as danger zones. That is, you can touch, have sex, and do anything to your partner, but not with your hands or mouth. It will complicate things, and there will be a distinct sense of unfulfillment that will absolutely be remedied later. Imagine that you want to grab, stimulate, or suck – you can't do any of these things! However, you're creative and resourceful, so you'll figure something else out, don't worry.

What are the other ways you can give sexual pleasure? You'll find out.

The second version of this game is to not touch the genitals at all, though you can do everything with all of your limbs and mouth. This is particularly frustrating and good at building tension because you want to escalate matters, but you are forced not to. On some level, you are reduced to dry humping like teenagers in the back of a car.

That's not such a bad thing, is it? Just make sure to adhere to the rule of not touching the genitals, and you will experience an amazing release afterwards. During the course of normal sex, we often move too quickly for anticipation to build. Keeping a sense of tension and anticipation will make the payoff that much sweeter.

Sweaty Mess Sex Games

Chapter 5. Foreplay Games

Now we're getting to the good stuff. Foreplay is the stage right before sex that directly builds up tension. For some of us, we define that in the baseball system – first base isn't foreplay, but second and third base are, while the home run of course is intercourse itself.

Some of us might say foreplay begins as soon as you begin touching when sex is the inevitable conclusion. Another definition? Foreplay is everything but the orgasm. You can ask one hundred people to define foreplay and get one hundred definitions. For the purposes of this book on sex games, foreplay is what gets you really riled up and yearning for actual intercourse. It gets you in the mood and builds tension until you're unable to hold it anymore.

Keep that in mind as you try these foreplay games out. If you do them properly, you may not last that long, but that's the point!

Clean and Shave

This is a highly erotic game because it puts you into roles. It's not quite role play, but it puts you into a lower position than your partner, and vice versa. The name sounds like you visiting a barber, but it's about how you will be serving your partner.

First, you are going to strip them naked and draw a hot bath for them. Imagine that you are an ancient Roman servant washing their master. You will soap them, shampoo their hair, and even use a sponge on them. Have them sit in the bath and clean them from head to toe, and try to make it as loving and sensual as possible. You can also do it in as cold and detached a manner as possible, which is the opposite sentiment and, to some, incredibly arousing.

Of course, pay special attention to the erogenous zones. The simple act of soaping up and lathering those areas should be very pleasurable for both of you. The psychological divide you create with essentially a master and a slave are also sexy, and are similar to the sentiment created in a BDSM relationship. This can be like dipping your toe into that deep, deep pool to see how you like it. The slave gains arousal from serving and being used, and the master gains arousal from power and control.

This takes another level when we get to the shave portion of this sex game.

After the bath, make sure to apply moisturizing lotion to your partner like you are massaging them, except in the genital region, because that's where you are going to shave and groom them.

Caution: *don't use any type of razor near the genitals unless you are supremely comfortable and have experience handling them.* If you have any doubt, it's best to start with an electric shaver, similar to one you might use for haircuts and shaving facial hair. After you groom to your liking (something different from their normal pubic haircut is always going to be more arousing and sexy), wash their hair off, and moisturize their genitals with lotion.

Stay in your roles as you begin to pleasure them.

The Dry Hump

This is a battle of willpower and the competition will always create intense lust.

Here's how it works. Both of you start off in your underwear, and your goal is to make your partner ask for sex or initiate it. Penetration, to be exact.

To accomplish this goal, both of you will do your best to arouse the other person as much as possible, but over the underwear. You can do anything else, but both of your underwear has to stay on the entire time. Think of it like a cloth chastity belt that you both have to work around.

You will be dry humping copiously, as well as soaking the underwear with saliva and other bodily fluids. You can use your mouth, hands, vibrators, and spanking paddle. You may even achieve orgasm without having to take off your underwear.

The game ends when the underwear comes off – the person who removes or moves it is the loser. As with many of these games, but loser is actually a winner in the ensuing sex. This game is great because you build tension to the point where you can almost beg for sex, and beg for the foreplay to be over. You'll be either soaked or rock-hard, and it's easy to imagine that two strips of thin cloth aren't going to keep you from further pleasure!

Just The Tip

This is similar to the previous sex game, but this time you are taking your underwear off. Whew! The rules are the same, and you are still the loser if you initiate or ask for actual penetrative sex.

However, this time the underwear is off, and you can also play with *tips*.

You may insert only the tip of your finger into her vagina. You may only take the tip of his penis into your mouth. You may insert only the tip of a penis into a vagina.

These are the ways you can tease your partner into grabbing you and shoving you deep inside, whatever the orifice. See who breaks first and can't control themselves.

It's a test of willpower, especially when the tip of the penis is sliding in and out of a vagina. Who can hold out longer? Who's moaning louder or moving their hips more? Turn your partner on as much as possible without going over the edge yourself. Again, the loser isn't really the loser in this game!

Read Out Loud

This game is great for those of us that love erotica (me!). As with everything else, it gives you a way to tease and constrain sexual tension until a certain point where neither of you can take it anymore.

Search online or pull out your favorite piece of erotica – in other words, a passage where the characters are having graphic, explicit sex. The more explicit the better, really.

You or your partner, preferably the partner with better self-control, are going to read the sex scene out loud slowly, and you are going to emulate exactly what's happening in the scene. Follow along with it, including the intercourse portion.

Try to set the scene beforehand and understand the characters in the scene and where the sex scene is. Stay in character and only use the erotica as your cue in what to do next. This is another minor form of role play mixed with listening to instructions.

If the character kisses the other passionately, take a small break and enact that passionate kiss. Emphasize and drag out each act that is described in the erotica. This is going to be a relatively slow pace, which is great for building sexual tension and wanting. The challenge here will be reading through the entire piece of erotica, beginning to end. Keep it up during intercourse, and especially during the orgasms for both partners. Wherever and whenever the erotica says either partner orgasms, make it so!

You've read out loud thousands of times in your life, but I have a feeling this one just might be a little different.

Senseless

This sex game requires just a couple of simple props: blindfolds and earplugs.

For the next fifteen minutes of foreplay, you are each going to be senseless. This means wearing blindfolds, earplugs, and you are not allowed to talk. All of your information about what's happening will come from touch and feel. No communication, just going at each other like primal beasts.

The lack of sight and hearing takes foreplay to a new level, because it heightens your sense of touch, and it is also incredibly sexy to guide through touch only. You aren't able to say what you want, so instead, you grab their body and put them in that position, or push their head down. It simultaneously allows you to take charge and be led.

The other reason this sex game is so great is because it's empowering. If you know your partner can't see or hear you, you will feel braver doing things you wouldn't otherwise. You'll have less fear of judgment because you won't have questioning eyes weighing on you, and not being able to speak helps you skip the step of asking and takes you straight into doing. If you wanted to try a new position or act, there's no more convenient time than this.

One more thing. You may not orgasm in these fifteen minutes. You must last until the blindfolds and earplugs come off. Only then may you orgasm.

One Pant Leg

This next game is great for mixing it up and introducing a bit of novelty into foreplay.

Ahead of time, you will decide which partner will keep all of their clothes on during foreplay and sex. In fact, during the whole act, the clothed partner must remain as clothed as possible while still being able to have sex. The other will be completely naked as normal.

Proceed to foreplay and sex as normal, keeping the same amount of clothing, or lack thereof, the entire time. Get creative and figure out how to make it work to your advantage.

Sensual Massage

You knew this had to be here somewhere!

The sensual massage is one of the most classic methods of foreplay. Just picture it: naked bodies, candlelight, relaxing music, and a slippery body for you to stroke.

First things first – you need massage oil to be most effective. Coconut oil does just as well if you don't want to go out and buy expensive massage oil. Have your partner strip naked and lie face down on the bed while you straddle them on top. You will be naked as well.

First, start out like a normal massage. Get into their knots and make them as relaxed as possible. Make them moan with pleasure at how you are kneading their muscles. Do this for at least ten minutes, then flip them over so they are lying on their backs.

Proceed as normally still, and give equal time to their muscles as well as their genitals.

Make sure you are both oiled up and slippery. Start to gradually give more attention and strokes to their genitals. After a certain point, your partner won't be able to control themselves and will beg you for sex. Make sure your genitals are oiled up as well, so your first thrusts will be smooth sailing.

Sweaty Mess Sex Games

Chapter 6. Challenge Games

What exactly is a challenge sex game?

It's where you are trying to accomplish a task during sex. It's usually going to be a task that involves some effort and focus, so it's challenging to complete both the task and a satisfying sex session. However, that doesn't mean we can't try and have fun in the process.

After all, it's through challenges and pushing ourselves to our limits that we find what we are capable of, and what we truly like. Above all else, it's just fun to try to turn sex into a game for you to conquer. As we all know, it's easy to get addicted to games that we haven't conquered yet, so these sex games may encourage you to have sex more frequently as well.

These aren't necessarily during foreplay or intercourse, they can be done and applied whenever you want to liven things up.

Lava Monster

Remember when you were a child and you played on the swings, there was a game where you had to stay off the gravel or tanbark? It consisted of you swinging from bar to bar, and making jumps from one area to the concrete and back.

Now, imagine that combined with sex. The floor (carpet, rug, wood, whatever you wish to define it as) has suddenly turned into steaming hot lava, and you can't touch it! You can have sex anywhere but the floor, but your task is to move from one room to the next.

You can take a maximum of three steps on the floor at a time, at which point you had better hop up on a table, counter, or chair and start having sex again. You only get three steps in between sex as well.

The more creative you get, the more fun this is. Start in the kitchen and work your way to your bed with only a couple of chairs and a rug to help you. How about figuring out positions that can work while one of you is standing, and the other is awkwardly twisted, trying to stay balanced? Or even walking through the house and stripping your clothes off, then having to follow that trail of clothing back to the bedroom without touching the floor underneath?

Remember, you can use more than just furniture. You can even, in desperation, grab a magazine or blanket from nearby and throw it on the floor to use. Be resourceful and have fun. It's best to start moving from just one room to another, and with plenty of objects in between. When you're ready for a bigger challenge, you can move across the house and back, taking different routes, using objects that only allow for one person to be stable at a time.

One Finger

This might be a challenge for some, and it might be extremely easy for others! The task here is to make your partner orgasm with just one finger. You take turns, and the one who can accomplish this the fastest wins. You can use other props, such as pornography, but your physical contact must be limited to one finger.

Men can finger, rub, and penetrate. You might think that the man has a distinct advantage in this because it's easier to focus on a clitoris as opposed to a penis with one finger.

That might be true, but there are plenty of ways women can stimulate a penis with one finger. Just focus on the crown of the penis, or if your fingers are long enough, wrap it around for a one-finger handjob. If it continues to be too unbalanced, simply move the goalposts, where victory for the man means two orgasms, and victory for a woman means only one orgasm.

This will again force you to be creative and resourceful and truly think, "How can I make an orgasm happen within these boundaries?" After all, necessity is the mother of invention, and you just might be inventing some unorthodox ways to create mutual pleasure.

Chase That Feeling

This sex game is a game of nostalgia and trying to recapture previous emotional and physical highs.

Each partner is going to think about the best sex they've ever had as a couple – with that specific partner. Then, you will think back to all of the circumstances surrounding it – what, where, when, why, how. Try to recall as much detail as possible about it, even if you fill in gaps with guesses.

You and your partner's best sex moments may not match, but that's okay. That just means you will take turns.

After you have filled in all the details about that moment, you will try to reproduce that sexual encounter as closely as possible with what you've taken note of.

If it was on the beach and you're far from the beach, use some sunscreen, put on ocean sounds, and sit on a towel on the ground. It if was in your car, drive your car to a dark alley (or maybe just your backyard) and do the deed there, playing the same music and wearing the same clothes. If it was in your bed after a long date, visit that same restaurant and order the same dishes before going home to do the dirty.

Just try to get the setting as similar as possible. This turns this game into a fun planning event for you two as well, because it will make you work together to build the scene.

As for the actual sex itself, try to emulate that too! Who made the first move, what happened, what positions you were in, and how penetration was first made. You can try to emulate the positions you used, and how and where you orgasmed as well, if you remember that. Did they do anything special that turned you on or surprised you? Did you cuddle afterwards and gear up for round two or did you have to hide from your partner's parents?

You are chasing an old memory, but simultaneously creating a new one, and perhaps even improving on it.

Name It

This sex game will test your sense of intuition.

Both of you will be naked. One partner will be blindfolded, and the other will be in charge of the game. The partner in charge will pleasure the blindfolded partner with an object for up to sixty seconds, and the receiver has three attempts to guess what the object is.

If the receiver is correct within those three attempts, then they are rewarded with whatever they want for sixty seconds. If they are wrong, however, they must change roles and blindfold the other partner. It will be more fun if you get creative and don't use sex toys. Instead, you can use household objects, food, clothing, unconventional parts of your body, or even sports equipment. You are only limited by your creativity what can you use to pleasure your partner!

Keep Rhythm

Music during sex is almost always a plus to set the mood and make it feel like you are in a world of your own.

This game takes it to the next level by requiring you to have sex to the beat of the song that is playing. To do this most effectively, look up a playlist on YouTube that changes songs or beats every sixty seconds. You can also set your normal music playlist to shuffle if that's easier for you. Just make sure that the songs played after one another are random and different in speed and rhythm.

Start this playlist when you begin foreplay, but you should really start paying attention when you start intercourse. Keep the beat of the music, stay in rhythm, and adapt when the song changes every minute. This will give you plenty of variety to play with, and make sure that the male and female have equal time on top, because the partner on top is essentially who controls the rhythm.

It would probably be worth your time to build a playlist of 60-second snippets ahead of time, just to ensure that the songs are of very different rhythms and speeds. For example, songs from salsa, techno, tango, and country are all very different and will make you move in a very different way. At the very least, you might discover new music that you like.

Staring Contest

This is a game you probably played as a child or with your cat, but it takes on a whole new meaning here.

This is mostly for use during intercourse. In this game, you and your partner will only have sex in positions where you can maintain eye contact. Missionary, cowgirl, side, whatever variations you wish to swivel into. Do your best to maintain eye contact the whole time, and don't break it unless you have to.

The first partner to look away or break eye contact loses a point. This game operates on a points system where the partner who has the higher score (whoever breaks eye contact the least) gets to choose a reward.

The staring contest sex game is great for a couple of reasons. First, it makes you feel more connected as a couple. That's what sustained eye contact can do, and it can make you feel like you can feel their soul, as well as their body. You may notice this session turns out to be more intense than normal for this very reason. Second, this becomes more difficult the closer we get to orgasm – we feel the need to look away or close our eyes. That adds a fun wrinkle, and puts you both on an even playing field!

Public Groping

We all have a little bit of an exhibitionist in us.

This game works by trying to touch your partner sexually as many times as possible in public.

The scoring system is as follows:

Grope penis/vagina over clothes: 1 point
Grope penis/vagina under clothes: 2 points
Grope penis/vagina over clothes for 5 seconds: 3 points
Grope penis/vagina under clothes for 5 seconds: 4 points
Oral under clothes (must be at least 3 seconds long): 6 points

You can see what you might want to prioritize if you want to maximize points! If you are caught, meaning a member of the public sees what you are doing, then you don't get the points. You can feel free to add different levels if the above is too daring or too tame for you.

Set the boundaries of this game to be an entire day, a trip to the mall, an errand, or out to lunch. Just make sure to agree on it beforehand so you don't end up fondling your partner in front of their parents.

Here's where it gets better: even though you are competing, you can both wear clothing that makes this easier for both of you. Skirts without underwear, elastic waistlines, short shorts, large baggy shirts, huge purses, big hats, and so on. If that feels too risky still, you can even alter your clothes to make it easier, such as cutting holes near the crotch or in pockets or pants so your partner can grope you in secret.

It will also help to think about specific locations where you can do this, such as photo booths, cars, dark corners, public restrooms, behind buildings, dressing rooms, and so on.

Public Groping can start as innocent fun, but can turn super hot and build incredible sexual tension, forcing you to race home unexpectedly from the gym because you are too aroused. Errands never looked so good!

Chapter 7. Sexy Funny Games

Some of you might find it difficult to be sexy, romantic, or passionate all of the time. Even I grow tired of it sometimes! It's not that it's not in us, but we sometimes feel like we need a change of pace, and sometimes we just need to inject more fun and joy into our sex lives.

After all, this is a book about games, right? People play games to have more fun and get more pleasure out of things. Sure, they also do it because it helps people initiate sex and spark more sexual interest from their partners, but it all comes together because there is a baseline of fun underlying everything.

<u>Use The Mirror</u>

This game is one we can all do easily because we all have mirrors in our homes. Whether this occurs in the bathroom or bedroom doesn't matter.

You are going to have sex doggy style in front of the mirror so both of you are facing it, and you are both looking at each other. Where does this turn funny?

You are both going to do your best to make the other person break character and start laughing by your facial expressions. In other words, the game is to use your face to make your partner laugh. The smaller version is to make your partner crack a smile. Typically, you would use goofy faces, and I remember a friend telling me that she hid a werewolf mask and put it on during this game and was declared the winner for the decade.

The winner of this game gets to dictate the rest of the sexual encounter, and be serviced in exactly the way they like.

Be The Star

This sex game works in conjunction with porn. The aim is to be the most exaggerated, absurd version of a porn star that you see and hear.

Make the same facial expressions, moan just as ridiculously, and use all the same dirty talk phrases that you hear. Scream like you never have before, and try to keep a straight face during all of this. This applies to both males and females.

Follow along with all the positions as you can, but the important part is to mimic exactly what you hear. You might have to search a bit to make sure the video you are watching is particularly vocal.

This isn't just fun, it can broaden your horizons substantially. When you discover that you are able to say these things, sometimes seriously, and sometimes even erotically, your boundaries have just been expanded. If you could only mutter "I like it," on Monday, and are forced to scream, "Fuck me in my dirty anus, master!" on Tuesday, you can imagine how much more you might be able to say on Wednesday.

In this sex game, you get to feel like you are a porn star and living out a fantasy. This is a minor form of role play that lets you inhabit someone else's body and lack of inhibitions. Scream at the top of your lungs and walk around the next day with the knowledge of what you can do!

Best Kisses

Do an Internet search for the following right now: "best movie kisses."

What do you come up with? That's what you're going to re-enact with your partner!

For example, a kiss from the movie *The Notebook* may have popped up. You are going to watch it with your partner, emulate the circumstances, and then emulate the passionate kiss itself. That particular kiss is in the rain, so you could even do it in the rain, or in the shower, or under a hose. To repeat, you want to try to use all of the elements that you see in the kissing scene.

Before you start this game, find a few kisses that run the gamut, from conservative to intensely passionate. Take a few minutes to

82

discuss how to approach each kiss and plan for it. They might even necessitate an outfit change! There's no winner or loser in this game, you are just working together to recreate something that you've seen in movies or television.

Note that you can do this with all sorts of scenes from movies and media. Foreplay scenes, sex scenes, even romantic flirting scenes.

Wrestle You For It

It's a battle! You are wrestling to steal a kiss on the lips from your partner.

Here's how it works in more detail: you are trying to pin your partner or otherwise get a kiss on the lips from them however possible. This is going to involve physically sneaking around or dominating your partner. If there is a big size disparity between you two, you can give the bigger or stronger partner a handicap, such as only using one arm or one leg.

There will be three rounds. One partner will be on top, and the other on bottom – you can define that as you wish for these purposes. These positions will alternate every round. There is no time limit. A round will only end when someone has gotten a kiss (and a point).

It's a best-of-three scenario! In other words, the first partner to secure two kisses is the winner, and the loser must immediately give oral to the winner.

Drawing Contest

I dare you to keep a straight face during this sex game!

The first step is to go to a store and purchase some washable markers. You're going to have a good, old fashioned draw-off. Strip down naked, and sit with your legs open across from each other.

Yep, you're going to be drawing there. Each partner has fifteen minutes to draw something on and around the genitals. Use your creativity! It can be absolutely anything – the penis can be an elephant's trunk, you can draw a mountain scene on the vagina, you can draw eyes on the penis head, you can give the vagina teeth. The only limits are your imagination. Use different colors, shading textures, you can even use as much of their body as you want, so long as it includes the actual genitals.

After both of you are done, a winner will be declared. The winner wins being washed and cleaned by the loser.

Chapter 8. Dirty Talk

Dirty talk? Yeah, it definitely belongs in a book about sex games! They accomplish the same goal of introducing something novel to a sexual relationship and making it more intense.

Dirty talk faces many obstacles from people. People feel too self-conscious, they feel "weird," or they just plain don't know what to say.

Just in case you want some guidelines (these are written from the perspective of a man because it's what I tell my male clients most often):

First, tell her what you want to do with her and be specific. For example, "I'm going to bend you over like a bad girl."

Second, tell her what you want her to do to you and be specific. For example, "I want you to get on your knees and ask me what I want."

Third, brush up on your dirty vocabulary and make sure that you can say filthy words without giggling or cracking a smile.

Finally, ask her questions that you know the answer will be "yes" to. For example, "You like when I pull your hair hard?"

It can be tough to simply open your mouth and utter those things. Logic has nothing to do it with it, and self-consciousness and potential judgment everything.

We can have all the justification in the world to do something, but that's not what determines our actions in daily life... as many of us are far too familiar with.

Even if I give you the perfect phrases to whisper, they will be useless until you can actually work up to whispering or shouting them during orgasm.

Simply put, the first time you try anything new, you will feel that self-consciousness and adrenaline rush of uncertainty. It is unavoidable. But there are steps you can take to reduce those feelings and turn them into excitement and arousal.

Hell, you might even skip over a couple of the following steps because you've acclimated more quickly than you expected – and that's what I find with most people. The important thing here is that everyone moves along at their own pace of comfort, and no one can be expected to follow someone else's and move together exactly.

So if your partner is lagging, guess what... go back and help them!

Step one – bring it up innocently

First, talk about dirty talk with your partner. Bring it up innocuously and gauge their reaction to it. Tell them that a friend told you about it, and you were intrigued, so that the burden can be blamed on someone else. Or say that you read an article about it, saw a television piece on it, etc. You can also watch something together that has elements of dirty talk so the topic comes up independently of you.

Bringing it up this way gives you an out and plausible deniability so you can avoid self-consciousness and judgment. Your partner most likely will not be judging you, but this is an approach that helps you justify talking about it.

I would estimate that 99% of the time, your partner will be intrigued and agreeable to trying whatever you suggest in the name of spicing up bedroom relations. If they aren't, they might simply be in the same shoes you are – afraid of judgment and self-conscious about their sexuality. If that's the case, you need to move along slowly and emphasize that you are interested in exploring it.

You might need to bring the topic up more than once for it to truly implant in your partner's head.

If they are truly reluctant to give it a shot, there's not much you can do except continue to keep communication lines open and extoll the virtues of dirty talk.

Do *not* push them into something they don't want to try.

Step two – learn your vocabulary

Don't dive into using dirty talk during sex yet.

You need to focus on the two main components of dirty talk – *vocabulary, and action phrases*.

As you'll see, you will need to be comfortable and proficient with both of them. Get used to using various vocabulary words such as "cock," "pussy," "tight," "soaked," "fuck me" and so on. *Think* about how you can use them in your daily life to get over any prevailing stigma you might feel from them.

Roll them around your tongue and mouth them – you don't need to outright say or use them yet. You can do the same with action phrases such as "I'm going to," "spread yourself," "bend over," "pound me," and the like. Whisper them to yourself and become comfortable with them.

You are becoming a person who is a dirty talk expert, and that requires changing your mindset and expanding your comfort zones.

Make sure that you are also ridding yourself of your daily usage of lesser dirty talk words like "wiener," "dick," "vagina," and so on. Those are kiddy words. They have no place in dirty talk.

Step three – writing and typing it

Third, test these phrases and vocabulary out via text or instant messaging. Actually writing these out will be adrenaline-inducing for the first few times, but you'll find that the initial hurdle… is really the only hurdle there is. The first time is the hardest, and each time you use anything you'll be exponentially more comfortable with it. Once you see that there is no negative reaction, that's going to be a powerful piece of positive reinforcement to keep pushing the envelope!

If you need an intermediate step between steps two and three, I suggest seeking out an online chatroom geared towards cybersex and dirty talk. For some, this skirts a moral grey area, but it's in the name of love! Try out your phrases anonymously and without fear of retribution and judgment! The goal is just to get used to actually using them on someone, and seeing the proper context and reactions that people will have. You might even pick up a few tips while you're there.

Once you've mastered using your phrases and vocabulary via the written word, you can try trotting them out in person in the next step.

Step four – introduce outside of the bedroom

Fourth, now that you're comfortable with all the phrases and words and actually have used them to some degree, try using them in a joking manner with your partner *out loud… not during sex*. Take away the stigma and the embarrassment by saying everything with a wry smirk, and get used to saying the words and their reactions.

You'll get a chance for feedback, practice, and to discover what your partner particularly likes or does not like. Watch some amateur pornography for inspiration on how to use dirty talk naturally and organically. If you're still having trouble, try finding some audiobooks of erotica or erotic stories online – you can see exactly what kind of tone and inflection that you can use.

The goal in this step is to get used to saying the vocabulary and phrases with your partner orally to find out what they like and build comfort.

Step five – transition to sex

Finally, transition into the bedroom. At this point, you should have no issues saying that you want to say because you've already taken away the mystique of the words in other contexts. You should also realize at this point that there will be no judgment on your partner's part. This is key.

It will be slightly nerve-wracking because it is a new context, but you'll have these phrases at the tip of your tongue and instinctually realize when to use them for maximum arousal.

Start with moaning and groaning louder and more emphatically than normal.

Then continue by incorporating dirty talk phrases into your moaning and groaning. Practice makes perfect!

You may find that you have to do the majority of the leading and dirty talking when you first begin with your partner, so be prepared for it.

The wonderful part about dirty talk is that you have probably been playing a waiting game – that is, your partner didn't want to be the first person to bring it up, and is thankful that you did it. Discovering shared secret interests, especially those of the dirty nature, can be a huge aphrodisiac in itself.

The phrase "It's not what you say, but how you say it" has rarely mattered more than with dirty talk. I can feed you the phrases to use (and I will later), but there are a few guidelines that we have to cover in the delivery of your dirty talk. Of course, part of this is practice and realizing what works for you and your partner.

Delivery is key for dirty talk because of the overall mood and tone you are seeking to cultivate.

Here are some additional guidelines on dirty talk delivery:

1. Describe how they are making you feel by what they are doing to you in that moment. Make it personal, that they are the ones affecting you and only them.
2. Direct them – command, ask, beg, demand, or plead. Also, add "please" to many dirty talk phrases.
3. Narrate your actions. Tell them what you are doing, or what you are going to do to them.
4. Praise them. Be specific, and focus on their physical attributes. Many people's self-esteem is wrapped up in their physical appearance, so if you praise them, you are simultaneously building their confidence as well as dirty talking. When someone is more confident about their body and has high self-esteem, they'll be more likely to explore new thing and be open – this can only work in your favor.

5. Talk in terms of possessions. You are hers, she is yours. Your cock is hers, her pussy is yours. Etc.
6. You don't have to actually answer a question they pose in their dirty talk. Many are rhetorical. As long as you acknowledge it or even moan to it, that is sufficient.

And just to give you a nice start, here are 62 great dirty talk examples!

1. Don't stop pounding me
2. Make me scream
3. Your pussy is so warm/tight
4. Your cock is so hot/big
5. You're filling me up
6. Fuck me harder
7. You feel so tight
8. Right there
9. Deeper
10. Only you can fuck me like this
11. Only you know how I love it
12. Give me that cock/pussy
13. I'm going to fuck you until you break
14. May I come?
15. You make me feel so full
16. Fuck that feels so good
17. That cock feels so good in my pussy

18. That's my good/bad girl
19. Say my name
20. Flip over and spread your pussy
21. Look at me
22. You look amazing spread under me/bent over
23. Choke me
24. I love feeling you inside me
25. Do you like that?
26. You are so hot
27. You drive me wild
28. I want to make you cum
29. Make me cum
30. I'm going to watch you cum
31. You're so deep
32. Do you like it deep?
33. I need you
34. I've been thinking about this all day
35. You're going to make me cum so hard
36. You like when I spread for you?
37. I'm going to suck you until you come
38. Ride me harder
39. You're my naughty girl
40. Bend over, slut
41. I love fucking you
42. Lick it clean
43. I'm going to clean you clean
44. You're so hard inside me
45. Moan for me

46. You're driving me crazy
47. I'm going to fuck you until you can't walk
48. I'm so fucking wet
49. Beg me
50. You own me
51. Take it all
52. You're my fucktoy now
53. Make me your fucktoy
54. You can do anything you want to me
55. Fuck my cunt
56. Spread your pussy lips
57. Tell me what you want
58. You're making me shake
59. Fuck me raw
60. Fuck me from behind
61. Make it hurt
62. Do you have any idea what you're doing to me?

Sweaty Mess Sex Games

Chapter 9. Role Play and Fantasies

Role playing is when you pretend that you are someone else. That's the most basic definition I can give, but it obviously contains so much more.

People use role play to experience fantasies or scenarios that have always intrigued them, or been out of reach. For instance, sex with a new partner is extremely exciting, so why not role play that it's happening? It's as close as most of us will get to a new partner without actually switching partners!

Role playing capitalizes on common fantasies, sometimes power play, and above all else, allows you to be someone else and shed your notions of self-consciousness and judgment.

When you step into a role, you aren't yourself anymore. All of your actions and words are a result of the role. If you feel self-conscious about an action, never fear, because there won't be repercussions... it was the role.

If you are engaging in a naughty school girl role play fantasy, and you mention the word "daddy" one too many times or reference how you like to be fucked in the ass, don't worry! It was for the role. You're in an automatic safe zone. You may not have realized those desires in you before, and being able to experience and acknowledge them is the first step to better sex. That's impossible for many people without role play.

The number one rule for better role play is to stay in character! This means to stay in your role and not step out of it unless absolutely necessary. The entire purpose of role play is to create a character for yourself, and subsequently a fictitious relationship, so you must stay in character for full effect. I can't emphasize this enough. Try to refrain from an attack of the giggles or confused looks.

Here are some of the best role plays you can easily integrate into your sex life, starting tonight.

Strangers

This is a role play where you act like you don't know each other. Whether in private or in public, you have just met the other person – and they are taking on a different identity or role. For example, you might give yourself a different name and entire backstory while you're out at a bar waiting for your partner.

Continue to stay in these roles and backstories, with the only predictable part being that you will be flirtatious and attracted to your partner when you see them.

The key here is that you are both normal, different people, and you are essentially pretending to set yourself up for a one night stand, or torrid affair. The joy is in creating an alter ego, someone that you might like to be, to fulfill another type of fantasy. You can even talk about the scenario beforehand with your partner so there are no surprises. One can be a married man, and the other, a flirtatious bartender. You get the idea.

You can either go in blind, or agree beforehand what the roles will be. It might behoove you to start with setting boundaries at first, and then freestyle and wing it when you are more experienced and comfortable with this role play. Just go with the flow and expect that the strangers are looking for the exact same thing.

Man/Woman in Charge

Here, the roles you will be playing either have power or none at all. It might be a complete role reversal for you, or it might encourage you to take your tendencies to their absolute limit.

For example, a schoolgirl with a teacher, a cop with an inmate, a doctor with a patient, or even a real estate agent and a prospective buyer.

The point is that there is someone who has to listen to the other person, and that can be taken to the extreme. The party in power will demand more and more, while the powerless party can only listen, say yes, seek to please, and cannot dare to resist.

Other roles are: a boss and a secretary, a valet or driver with a rich client, or even a customer service rep with a demanding customer.

The purpose of these roles is for one party to make demands, and the other to comply. If you don't like that angle, then you can shift the purpose to be one of punishment – one party is angry with the service and seeks to punish the other (the powerless).

Another classic role play with a power differential is a concubine or slave with their master, and the concubine or slave is taking care of their every need, such as bathing them. Make it the role of one person to wash the bathe the other person in a tub, first focusing on actually washing, then onto caressing and teasing. Then, slowly, the master might take the role of commanding them to pleasure them, or it might be a forbidden fruit scenario where the slave is seizing an opportunity for naughty pleasure.

Fantasy Bowl

This is a sex game where both of you write down five secret fantasies of yours on five pieces of paper. Fold the pieces of paper up and drop them all into a bowl. There will be ten fantasies milling about in the bowl.

Now, this is the important part. You are going to mix the bowl and pick one out... BUT you are not going to focus on the sex. You are just going to talk about it, what turns you on about it, and how you feel about it. Turn off the lights, get under the sheets, strip down naked, and focus on discussing and talking about how stimulating it would be.

If your partner describes their fantasy to you, just listen to them. Have them demonstrate it, or demonstrate on them how it would feel and how you might want it. Before you even realize it, both of you will be really turned on. The darker the sexual fantasies, the more aroused both of you will feel.

Make sure to cultivate a safe space for the other person to be comfortable opening up to you, otherwise they will feel embarrassed and judged, which will instantly keep your sex vanilla for ages. That's why simply getting into bed with the lights off is effective for discussing what's in the fantasy bowl.

The Maid/Butler

This sex game is great for building tension. The way this works is that you are going to slip into the role of being a sexy (or naked) maid or butler for a few hours. It might help you to think of this as more of a personal slave like previously mentioned, but this variation has more plausible deniability. A maid or butler's main purpose is not to pleasure you, rather to take care of the home.

Whoever is in the maid or butler role, that's what they will do. They will, naked or barely clothed, perform light household tasks, including acts of service for you.

For example, they might dust the shelves, lightly scrub the bathtub, scrub the oven, re-arrange the kitchen cabinets, wash the car in a white t-shirt, or slide under a desk with their legs spread wide open.

Things involving bending over or that will put your body in a provocative or compromising position, get you wet with water, or put you into unnecessary contact with your master.

The reaction of the master will then be to attempt to seduce their maid or butler. The maid or butler may refuse at first and attempt to be "professional", but will ultimately be overcome with desire and arousal. Make sure the maid or butler puts up a fight that is ultimately tossed to the side.

Remember, stay in character! Next time you play this, reverse the roles and let your partner experience things from the opposite side.

Phone Sex Operator

This sex game takes place when you are apart, or at least in separate rooms of your home. If you are both in the same home, lock your respective doors so neither of you can spoil the rising sense of anticipation.

It's relatively simple. One of you is the caller and one of you is the phone sex operator. Use the stereotypical husky voice as you've heard in commercials. The operator will take charge of the phone call, and ask the caller what they like and how they like it. They will direct the conversation and add color to the caller's answers.

This may seem like it's more work for the phone sex operator, but luckily there's a chapter on dirty talk in this book to help out! You can follow some of the guidelines there to help you with being in charge of phone sex, including thinking out loud more, stating what you want, what they want, how they want it, and what turns them on. You'll find that this will be easier than normal small talk, because you won't be able to see their potentially judging face.

Make sure to imply that you are playing with yourself, and ask your partner over the phone to play with themselves as well during the call.

Do this for a period of at least ten minutes. Anything less and you might not settle into the roles or get into something hot and heavy. Anything more and you might not be able to take it anymore!

Orgasm Master

This sex game has a bit of a BDSM bend to it. That is, it's very much about control and power over someone and how that makes both parties feel.

Orgasm Master means that you have sole control over how and when your partner orgasms. Before the sexual encounter, one of you will be anointed the Orgasm Master. This will usually play out in two ways: you can force them to orgasm any time during the encounter, or you can deny them an orgasm at any point.

When you force them to orgasm, you are either commanding them to orgasm on command, or you are ruthlessly making them orgasm from your touch. This might be more applicable to women, as men cannot easily achieve multiple orgasms. To put it another way, the master has complete power over the slave's pleasure, and can tease them at will.

When you deny an orgasm, you tease them to the edge of orgasm, then back off suddenly so they are left unfulfilled. This is also known as edging. This can be incredibly frustrating, but also make them want you that much more. Just make sure you can accurately judge when your partner is about to orgasm, so you can back off in time, before the dreaded point of no return.

You can turn denying orgasms into a competition in two ways. The first way is to see who can be on the brink of orgasm for the longest amount of time when they are the slave. You will pleasure your partner right to the edge of orgasm, and see how long it takes for them to beg you for release, when they can't take it anymore. You can use a stopwatch for this, and the person who lasts the longest is the winner and receives a sexual reward of their choosing.

The second way is to see how many times you can bring your partner to the edge without them orgasming. This is when you are the master, and it's a measure of how skilled you are at teasing. How many times can you walk that thin line and make them almost orgasm?

Sweaty Mess Sex Games

Chapter 10. Props and toys

Although mental sex games, role playing, and teasing are all amazing for improved sex, there is something to be said for sex games that involve tools, props, and toys.

I don't mean sex toys, because that would be too easy, but toys such as cards, Jenga, blindfolds, dice, and other physical objects we can adapt to use for sexual purposes. After reading through this chapter, I hope you can look around your house with a new perspective. You can adapt practically anything for sexual purposes, it just takes some imagination and creativity.

Bossy Cards

This is a game where you only need a single deck of cards. I'm going to give you the instructions on how to use them in a way that's sexier and more direct than strip poker could ever be.

You simply take turns drawing cards, and the suite and number of each card will tell you what you need to do.

- Hearts are kissing
- Diamonds are a sensual massage with oil
- Clubs are using your hands for manual stimulation
- Spades are oral.

The number of the card multiplied by four is how many seconds you have to perform the act for.

For example, if you were to draw a four of clubs, then you have to give your partner a sixteen-second handjob. Quite short, but the point is not to orgasm. You are drawing cards to tease and stoke the furnace of your lust. Keep drawing until you reach the end of the deck – if you can.

If you draw two of the same numbered cards in a row, you get double damage. This means you have to double the amount of time you must perform your duty.

If you draw two face cards (jack, queen, or king) in a row, you get a reversal, which means that instead of you performing an act on your partner, they will perform it on you.

Finally, if you draw the cards with the same suite three times in a row, you get to pause the game for sixty seconds, and your partner will perform an act of your choice on you.

Reading

This game is the ultimate test of willpower.

One partner is the reader, and the other partner is the pleaser. The reader will read out loud a chapter from a non-sexual book that will take roughly five to ten minutes, while the pleaser must do anything within their power to throw them off of their reading. The pleaser's job is to throw them off track and make them stop reading completely, whether by teasing, orgasm, penetration, or any other sexual means. The reader's job of course is to finish the chapter as seamlessly as possible.

Let's see who can thwart the other! Once the chapter ends, or the reader orgasms, then it's time to switch roles and see how well you fare in the other position.

For the reader, it's about focusing and diverting your mind away from the obvious pleasures that are being done to you, and for the pleaser it's about teasing, imposing your will, and bringing someone to the edge of orgasm and back again, multiple times.

Sexy Dice

There are many ways to play with dice, so I will present you with two of my favorites. You only need one die, but ideally you have two that are each six-sided.

Let's work with the assumption that you have two dice. The first way to play is to have each die represent the following: a type of sex, and a location.

For example, here's what the TYPE die can represent:

1. Back massage
2. Kiss passionately for 60 seconds
3. Manual stimulation
4. Oral Sex
5. Missionary
6. Doggy

Here's an example of the LOCATION dice:

1. Bedroom
2. Sofa
3. Dinner Table
4. Backyard
5. The pool
6. Public

You simply roll the dice one at a time, and follow the instructions you are given. For example, if you roll a four and a five – you will be having missionary sex in or near the pool.

The second version is a little bit more tame. You assign the dice a body part, and an act which you will do for thirty seconds.

Finally, here's an example of what the BODY PART dice are:

1. Mouth

2. Nipples
3. Neck
4. Ass
5. Genital Region
6. Ears

Here's what the ACT dice can look like:

1. Kiss
2. Suck
3. Sensual Massage
4. Lick
5. Bite
6. Manually stimulate

For example, if you roll a three and a six, you would manually stimulate, tease, and caress your partner's ears with your fingers for thirty seconds. Then you switch and take turns until you can't take it any longer.

For both of these dice games, make sure to write out the rules on a piece of paper so you can easily refer to it and instantly know what to do after you see the results.

Tied Down

This is where we use ribbon or ties as a prop. Note — do not use rope if you aren't experienced with knots, as they can lead to a loss of circulation and worse consequences. Here, we are tying our partner's wrists together behind them, and their ankles apart, if possible. Ideally tie both, but you can make do quite easily with just the wrists. Don't forget to blindfold them as well, if possible.

You are now the master, and you have control over your partner. Your task is to sexually tease them, but don't have vaginal or oral sex with them. Make them want it. Make them beg for it.

They are not allowed to speak anything except two different words you will have agreed upon beforehand: a safe word and a begging word.

The safe word is when they want to stop being tied down for any reason at all. I repeat, when you hear the safe word, you must immediately stop, untie them, and take their blindfold off. Consider this a break of character and cause for stopping the sex game.

The begging word is what we're aiming for. It's the word to signal that they give up, and they no longer want to be teased. They just want sweet release. They want to fuck – forgetting being teased.

This is a competition in the sense that you want them to say their begging word as quickly as possible, and they want to withhold it as long as they can.

Switch Card

This game will require some sort of timer or playlist (you can search these on YouTube easily) that will alert you every sixty seconds, and a deck of cards.

Before sex, each of you will choose an adjective for how they would describe their most ideal sex. For example, tender, smooth, rough, passionate, rushed, loving, angry, caring, and so on. If you both have the same idea of ideal sex, choose an adjective that is sufficiently different from the one they chose. Don't come into this with the adjectives of loving and caring, because then the purpose of this game will be defeated.

Let's assume you have adjectives like rough and tender, which are opposites. You will draw a card every sixty seconds, and the card will determine which adjective you abide by for the foreplay or intercourse. Each partner will be assigned either red or black – the colors of the cards.

If the adjective I chose is rough, and I am assigned the color black, every time a black card is drawn, we get to have rough sex or foreplay for sixty seconds. Then, another card will be drawn, and if it happens to be red, then we will have tender sex or foreplay for sixty seconds. And so on until completion!

This might just give you an appreciation for different styles of sex and what your partner likes. The alternating nature of this game will also keep you on your toes, guessing what will come up. You don't know if or when your preferred style will come again, so you can make the most of it!

Sweaty Mess Sex Games

Chapter 11. Creative and Ingenious

This chapter contains some of the most
creative and ingenious sex games that I've
ever come across. They may require a tad bit
more thinking or open-mindedness, but that
doesn't mean they are any less pleasurable!

Strip Questions

The name says it all. Ask your partner
questions about yourself, and if they get them
wrong, they strip.

No cards needed, all that's needed is a brief
survey of your own sexual practices.

To make it even more fun and sexy, wear old
clothes while playing the game – that way,
instead of simply removing a piece of

clothing, you or your partner can tear if off you.

What kind of questions should you ask about yourself to your partner?

- What's my favorite position?
- Where do I like to come?
- How do I come the hardest?
- What's my favorite dirty talk phrase?
- What gets me wetter/harder than anything?
- When am I horniest?
- How do I like to be touched/stroked?
- Where on my body besides my genitals turns me on the most?
- What's my biggest kink that we've already done?
- What's my biggest kink we haven't done yet?
- What do I wish we did more of?
- What was our hottest sexual experience ever in my opinion?

As you can see, the side benefit of this game is that you'll have a lot of knowledge that you may not have had before. You'll learn about your partner's preferences and best sexual practices, as well as play a fun game that leads to you being naked!

Penis Professor

This game is going to be a bit like trivia, but with a much better reward at the end.

Note that this applies only if you have a partner with a penis. You'll see why shortly. You are going to ask your partner (that possesses a penis) where his penis would go if he were having:

- Femoral sex rubbing
- Gluteal sex rubbing
- Popliteal sex rubbing
- Spinal sex rubbing

And for each of these that he gets correctly, he gets to do it!

If you don't know the difference yourself, femoral is rubbing the penis between the thighs, gluteal is rubbing between the butt cheeks, popliteal is rubbing behind the half-bent knee, and spinal is rubbing between the neck and the shoulders. Sound appealing?

Make sure you use plenty of lube, and you commit to each of these until ejaculation. Alternatively, you can start with normal vaginal sex, and then ejaculate in any of these positions. Believe me, it's very possible, and could be quicker than you expect.

Icy Hot

Icy Hot introduces food into the bedroom! Why not combine food and sex, two of my favorite things? Sometimes it can get messy, but the end result is often well worth the mess.

Icy Hot involves collecting two types of food: very cold, and very warm. You might want to shoot for three types of each food. For example, cold foods could be ice cream, champagne, ice chips, chilled strawberries, or chilled menthol gum. Warm foods could be melted chocolate, warm honey, or warm cider. Note that you should clean your personal areas very thoroughly before and after this game, otherwise you could end up with something nasty growing in an area where the sun doesn't shine.

Next, before your partner is able to see the foods or see what you are intending to do, blindfold them. Tell them you are going to treat them to oral, and you're in the mood for dessert, and their only job is to guess what you're using.

Take a spoonful or scoop into your mouth and start to perform oral sex very slowly and sensually. Make sure to run the food across their genitals so they can feel the different textures. Alternate between cold and hot foods for maximum effect, and don't tell them which is coming next. They are going to go wild at the change in sensation. It's a combination of being blindfolded, being surprised, and anticipation.

Next, you can switch to something completely different ... like some warm honey. The change should surprise your man, but more importantly it will make for a completely different sensation. Vary the amount of time you spend with each food, and keep them guessing. The shock to the system of cold versus warm is going to be extremely arousing and overload their senses.

Slippery Slide

There's nothing more erotic and hot than when you and your partner are both slippery with sweat and other fluids, and drenched from head to toe. It feels like the very definition of animalistic passion.

Now, the easiest way to do this is to have sex in a sauna, but that's essentially impossible unless you have a sauna built into your home. Besides, you'd have to have sex standing the entire time, because all the surfaces would be too hot for you to lie down on or touch.

The next best thing is to lay a couple of towels down in your bathroom floor, turn the shower on high, and close the door. This is going to trap the steam inside, and soon you'll have your very own sauna. Your bodies will start to get coated with sweat, and another bonus of the steamy environment is that your genitals will be already be half engorged from the heat. Just to make sure you are as slippery as possible, coat both of your bodies with coconut oil.

The next step is easy. Go to town on each other. Notice how erotic it feels when your bodies slide together, and how easy penetration is when you're soaked all over. It just creates the feeling that you are fucking like passionate animals. This might be less of a game and just a way to have really steamy sex (pun intended).

Litterbug

This game is called Litterbug due to the fact that you will be leaving notes all around your house for your partner to find. It's more a long-term game that can take weeks or months to finish.

This differs from the earlier Note Master sex game in that the notes are very action-oriented. They might be things to do immediately, or at the next sexual encounter. There are only a few rules:

1. If you see a note, you must open it immediately. If it demands that you do something at that moment, you must do it. No postponing.
2. Start with twenty notes each, half about immediate tasks (take two dirty pictures for me right now) and half about the next sexual encounter (next

time during sex, don't let me fuck you until you make yourself come in front of me).
3. When a note of yours is found, write and hide another one.

Sounds easy, right? Here are some samples of what you can write on the notes:

1. Immediately sneak away and send me three naughty pictures.
2. Wherever I am right now, find me and go down on me.
3. Make our bedroom a seduction lair and put on your sexiest underwear.
4. Come over to me right now and straddle and ride my face.
5. Next time we are in public, we can't go home until we both get to third base (oral).
6. Make your underwear wet right now and come give it to me.
7. Next time we fuck, I want you to face fuck me until you come.

You get the idea! There's another variation you can play on this that doesn't depend on pieces of paper.

You can use your phone to auto-schedule texts to send to your partner. If your phone doesn't have that capability, you can certainly auto-schedule emails. Compose and schedule these messages all on one day, and five at random times during the next week. Hopefully you will forget you even sent them, and it will be a nice surprise for both of you when they get the message, and are suddenly amazingly aroused.

By the way, if you live near or with other people, you may want to make sure that they don't stumble across your notes. You can come up with a code for them! You can put numbers on the notes, and they can tell you they found a certain number, and you can tell them what it means.

Sweaty Mess Sex Games

Chapter 12. My Personal Favorites

Now's the time for me to talk about my
personal favorite sex games to get you
titillated, teased, and orgasmic. It's not a sign
that the others are lacking. I've done all of
them at certain points, and I've only included
sex games in this book that are realistic and
sexy, not tedious or overly complex.

Coin Flip

All you need for this game is a coin. Nothing
could be simpler.

You both call a side of the coin and flip it. If it
lands on the side your partner calls (you lose),
you have to perform oral sex on them for a
period of two minutes. If it lands on the side
you call (you win), your partner has to

perform oral sex on you for two minutes. Keep flipping the coin and abiding by the result.

If you flip your side three times in a row, instead of oral sex, you now get to have intercourse for two minutes instead. After the time is up, you have to dismount and keep flipping the coin, if you can resist!

This game is the perfect combination of arousing yet frustrating, because you are forced to stop every two minutes – at least momentarily for a coin toss. If you continue to lose the coin flip, you become desperate to have it go in your favor, even though two minutes isn't that much time. It's also interesting because on one hand, you are rooting against your partner, even if you enjoy pleasing them. On the other hand, you are also rooting for your partner, because intercourse is probably the ultimate goal that you want more of. You are both competitors and teammates, which makes this game even more fun.

How does this end? When one of you can no longer control yourself.

Two Minutes in Heaven

This is similar to another game, but the premise is that you have two minutes to make your partner orgasm in any way possible.

After two minutes, it's your partner's turn to do the same thing! You are taking turns trying to get each other off.

Set an alarm to go off exactly every two minutes, and you can stay focused on the task at hand. You can use all of the weapons in your arsenal, including sex toys and other props.

This is great because it's extremely simple, and we all know some sex games are just too complex to adhere to in the heat of the moment. Two minutes is a carefully chosen amount of time: it's short enough so that your arousal will only grow, and it's long enough to make an impact and create an orgasm.

This game is also a competition. The loser is the person that orgasms first, and they then must give the winner an orgasm by any method of the winner's choosing. I love this sex game so much because it fires up my competitive juices and lets me play without restrictions on what I can do. Time is the only barrier, but that's easily overcome when you know what gets your partner off.

This game might not be great if one of you orgasms much more easily than the other, but in that case, you can do it as two orgasms versus one.

Truth or Dare

Good old truth or dare! You knew this had to make an appearance. It's a snap to adapt this child's game to naughty, kinky sex.

All you need to do is keep the questions focused on sex, sexual acts, and sexual fantasies... and impose a three-minute limit on each dare. This keeps a teasing overtone to everything and allows the game to continue. Talking about these topics in a way that you never would otherwise arouses people's appetites and instantly gets you in the mood.

What truths or dares can you ask?

- I dare you to [sexual act]

- When did you first want to fuck me?
- I dare you to [something exhibitionist]
- When did you come hardest with me?
- I dare you to [something challenging with their genitals]
- How do you like to be fucked by me? What position?
- I dare you to lick my nipples for sixty seconds.
- Do you like when I'm louder or quieter during sex?
- I dare you to demonstrate and show me how you like to be pleasured.
- What is your favorite song to have sex to?
- I dare you to give me a sixty second lap dance with heels.
- How tight/big did you think I would be?
- I dare you to suck on my toes.
- What gives you the most goosebumps or chills on your spine sexually?
- I dare you to bite from my feet up to my neck.

The only rule here is that you must be creative. Write these questions down beforehand so you don't run into roadblocks and pauses where you must think of the next thing to say.

They don't need to be dares per se, just things you would like done to you for sexual pleasure. This game can take a sexy angle, or a funny and novel angle. I love this game because I love being creative and pushing people's boundaries. At some point it may not even be about the sex, it's just about having sex while naked.

Hot Dog Buns

There are just a few features on a female that resemble hot dog buns, aren't there?

You have the lips, the buttocks, the external labia, and the breasts.

For the purposes of this game, you are going to treat all of these physical features just like hot dog buns. The male is going to rub and slide his cock between these lips, with absolutely no penetration of any type allowed. Make sure that you use plenty of lube, natural or not, to keep everything slippery and hot.

The most fun version of this game might be using the woman's labia as she rides the man, as she can also get pleasure from that as the cock rubs her clitoris. Imagine that she is riding just like the man's cock is inside of her. This becomes a game of who will come first, and who can resist harder than the other. It is the ultimate tease for both with the possibility of orgasm dangling right above them.

Just to emphasize, make sure both the cock and whatever hot dog buns you are using are slippery, wet, juicy, and ready. Absolutely no penetration, and focus on the task at hand. It's a tease but still pretty damn satisfying.

The Photographer

This is a game that you don't need a good camera for. You can just use a phone, even a terrible quality camera phone. After all, it's not really about the pictures themselves.

The photographer is in charge of putting a photo shoot together with the model. In preparation, gather a few sexy outfits and really commit to trying to look your best and sexiest. It's a good idea to ask your partner what they would like to see you in, because they will be able to keep the pictures for later.

Next, have the photographer arrange the model into the most arousing, pleasing, or sexy poses. It seems that you will have a better view if the model was naked, so direct them to strip. Get closer and closer with your camera, and then ask the model to start touching themselves for the camera. It's now a very different type of photo shoot.

Then, move closer and insist that you need pictures of you two together. Start foreplay and oral, and keep taking pictures, with the occasional video. At this point, you might find it difficult to hold onto your phone, but do it for as long as possible so you can go over these after you're done!

The Sleeper

This game just might be my favorite of all. This will vary from person to person, but I simply love getting woken up in the middle of the night to have sex. It's my favorite way to wake up, and I don't mind losing the sleep at all.

First, you have to clear this with your partner. You must ensure that they are okay with the fact that you will be waking them up in the middle of the night for a sexy tryst. Tell them it will only take about thirty minutes of their sleep, because let's face it, you'll also be tired. Luckily, an orgasm is the world's best form of tranquilizer, so you'll be asleep in no time afterward.

This game involves setting yourself an alarm, but trying to make sure that it doesn't wake your partner up. You want your touch to do that. If you've succeeded on this front, then start with light caresses on their crotch. Start stroking them more and more, but lightly so as not to wake them up. Slide inside their underwear and start touching them, and you'll find that they just might get physically aroused before they even wake up.

The ideal situation is for them to wake up while you are having intercourse, or the moment just before. Then, they can basically skip the foreplay and just arrive for the good stuff!

Again, you must make sure that they will be okay with this type of game.

Chapter 13. 60 Questions and Requests

There are three ways to use the information in this chapter.

First, you can use the following requests and questions you can use to supplement your games. In case you run out of things to say or your mind goes blank, you can just flip to this chapter and you have an entire archive of what to say.

Second, you can use this chapter directly to engage in a deeply sexual and arousing conversation.

Finally, if you have the paperback version of the book, you can actually cut them out as little cards and drop them into a bowl that you can draw out of later.

1. What, if done right before orgasm, will

   make it one of the best you've ever had?

2. Kiss your way down the front of my neck,

   down through my crotch, and then back

   up my spine.

3. Perform oral sex on my hand and show me

   exactly how you like it.

4. In what circumstances would you prefer to

   skip foreplay?

5. Would you prefer to be completely silent

   or incredibly loud during sex?

6. What turns you on to see in public?

7. Show me how you would try to seduce me

   into bed for the first time.

8. Would you have sex with me in a dressing

   room or public restroom?

9. Go into the next room and you have 2

   minutes to take 3 sexy photos. Send them

   to me.

10. Where would you most like to have sex

    that we have not yet?

11. Take a picture of us kissing passionately.

12. What is your most embarrassing moment

    during sex?

13. Film yourself orgasming for me tomorrow

    before noon.

14. What dirty talk phrase immediately turns

    you on?

15. Tell me about our last sexual encounter in

    as much detail as possible.

16. Do anything you want with me for the

    next 60 seconds.

17. What position or act would you like to do

    more of?

18. Kiss me for 40 seconds.

19. What do you like to hear me say during

    sex?

20. Nibble your name onto my back and neck.

21. Nibble my ears for 20 seconds each.

22. Describe what it's like to have sex with

    me.

23. Put a blindfold on me and run a feather or

    piece of cloth across my bare chest and

    thighs.

24. Begin touching yourself and continue for

    the remainder of this game.

25. Make your mouth hot with a warm liquid

    and then give oral.

26. Make your mouth cold with ice and then

    give oral.

27. Reenact a random porn scene you find

    right now by going to pornhub.com, typing

    a random letter, and then choosing the 8th

    video.

28. Download a Kama Sutra app on your

phone and find three positions you want

to try next time.

29. Eat a banana in the sexiest way possible

and keep a straight face.

30. Act like a submissive for the next 2

minutes.

31. Act like a master/dom for the next 2

minutes.

32. Strip naked and take a walk around the

    block.

33. Groom my pubic region.

34. Put Icy Hot or Ben Gay on your nipples.

35. Give me a hickey on my ass cheek.

36. Pretend to have a VERY loud and intense

    orgasm.

37. Name all the sex toys you have ever used.

38. What is the shortest amount of time it can

    take you to orgasm?

39. Drip honey (or chocolate or anything else)

onto my chest and lick it off.

40. Give me a 3 minute massage.

41. If you could receive anything sex-related

as a present, what would it be?

42. Let's reenact a piece of written erotica

right now.

43. Would you rather have sex with someone

watch, or watch people have sex?

44. Which Disney character or cartoon is most

sexually attractive to you?

45. No underwear for the rest of the day for

you.

46. Do a cartwheel naked.

47. What is your favorite type of porn?

48. When did you last masturbate?

49. What is the first thing you would do if you

could change genders for a day?

50. Would you prefer: a partner with a

horrible body but great face, or great body

and horrible face?

51. Switch clothing – whatever fits.

52. Show me the most sensitive part of your

body.

53. What is your sexual brag about your

abilities?

54. Describe exactly how your orgasms feel.

55. What would your stripper theme song be?

56. Unwrap a piece of candy in your mouth.

57. Both of you will take your bottoms off and

start spooning immediately.

58. Drip ice water over your partner's naked

body.

59. Drip candle wax over your partner's naked

chest.

60. Give five minutes of oral right now.

Sweaty Mess Sex Games

Glossary

Switch Card

Made in the USA
Columbia, SC
06 July 2020

13449952R00089